FLORA, FAUNA, BOTANICALS, AND BEES

Sticker, Color & Activity Book

chartwell
books

Quarto

© 2024 Quarto Publishing Group USA Inc.

This edition published in 2024 by Chartwell Books,
an imprint of The Quarto Group
142 West 36th Street, 4th Floor
New York, NY 10018 USA
T (212) 779-4972 F (212) 779-6058
www.Quarto.com

Contains content originally published as *Creative Candle Making* in
2019 by becker&mayer! books, an imprint of The Quarto Group, 142
West 36th Street, 4th Floor, New York, NY 10018 USA.

10 9 8 7 6 5 4 3 2 1

Chartwell titles are also available at discount for retail, wholesale,
promotional, and bulk purchase. For details, contact the Special Sales
Manager by email at specialsales@quarto.com or by mail at The Quarto
Group, Attn: Special Sales Manager, 100 Cummings Center Suite 265D,
Beverly, MA 01915, USA.

ISBN: 978-0-7858-4544-7

Publisher: Wendy Friedman
Senior Publishing Manager: Meredith Mennitt
Editor: Jennifer Kushnier
Designer: Angelika Piwowarczyk
Image credits: Shutterstock

Printed in China

CELEBRATE THE
diversity of life ON EARTH!

With *Flora, Fauna, Botanicals, and Bees Sticker, Color &
Activity Book*, you can take a closer look at the things
that are living all around you—that's *more than 2
million* non-plant species (fauna) and nearly 400,000
plants (flora).

These numbers merely scratch the surface.
Estimates vary, but that figure could actually
be millions—if not *billions*—of lifeforms on the
planet that have yet to be identified. While this
figure might be alarming in scope, it's not hard to
understand how it's possible. With better equipment
to help explore the deepest ocean trenches, the
densest jungles, and the most remote arctic regions,
we're able to find more organisms than ever before
reported.

But let's not forget about Charles Darwin. His
theory of natural selection put forth the idea that
all life today came from a few simple organisms that
evolved over millennia, weeding out the weak, and
promoting the best and strongest traits that helped
them adapt to the changing environment. So it's
only natural that we've not only found more species,
but there are more species to find.

Now you can get into the spirit of scientific discovery and partake in some less-scientifically-rigorous activities. Feast your eyes on the 500+ elaborate stickers featuring all manner of flora, fauna, botanicals, and bees. Use them to decorate envelopes, gift wrap, letters, scrapbooks, photo albums, and more! There are also inspiring quotes from naturalists and writers on the backs of the sticker pages.

To further relax and add fun to your free time, flip through the beautiful coloring pages depicting line-drawn art as well as the variety of puzzles, mazes, trivia, and matching games. Then try your hand at candle-making, flower drying, or making flower-infused syrups and vinegars with the instructions included in the book.

With so much to look at, so many things to do, and so much enjoyment to be had in these pages, *Flora, Fauna, Botanicals, and Bees Sticker, Color & Activity Book* is the perfect book to have on hand when a free moment strikes—or whenever the mood is right. Whether you're a sticker lover, scrapbooker, crafter, colorer, puzzler, or nature enthusiast, you're sure to find something unique in this treasure trove of natural beauty!

Match the Mammals!

A group of animals is often called a herd, but did you know that groups of different species go by very diverse names? See how many you can guess correctly.

Squirrels

Sloth

Pigs

Skulk

Journey, tower

Tigers

Giraffes

Ambush, streak

Colony

Foxes

Bears

Dazzle, zeal

Clowder

Zebras

Dray, scurry

Lemurs

Drift, drove

Cats

Mob

Goats

Conspiracy

Kangaroos

Trip

Rabbits

answers on the next page

Match the Mammals!

(answer key)

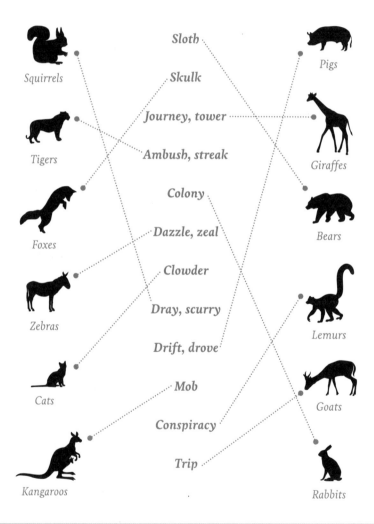

Squirrels

Tigers

Foxes

Zebras

Cats

Kangaroos

Sloth

Skulk

Journey, tower

Ambush, streak

Colony

Dazzle, zeal

Clowder

Dray, scurry

Drift, drove

Mob

Conspiracy

Trip

Pigs

Giraffes

Bears

Lemurs

Goats

Rabbits

solution on page 161

solution on page 161

solution on page 162

solution on page 162

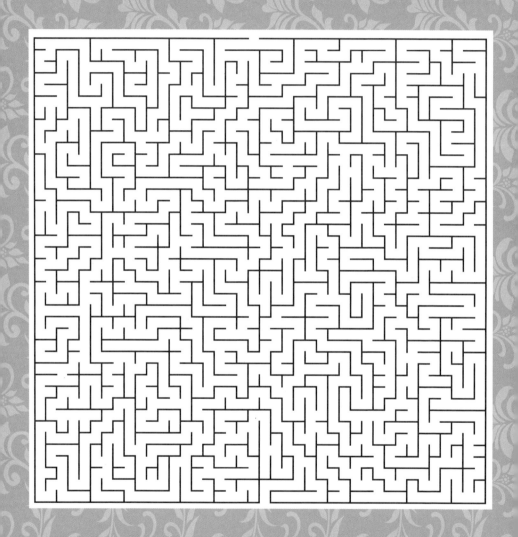

solution on page 163

solution on page 163

solution on page 164

solution on page 164

solution on page 165

"The world needs all you can give."

E. O. Wilson

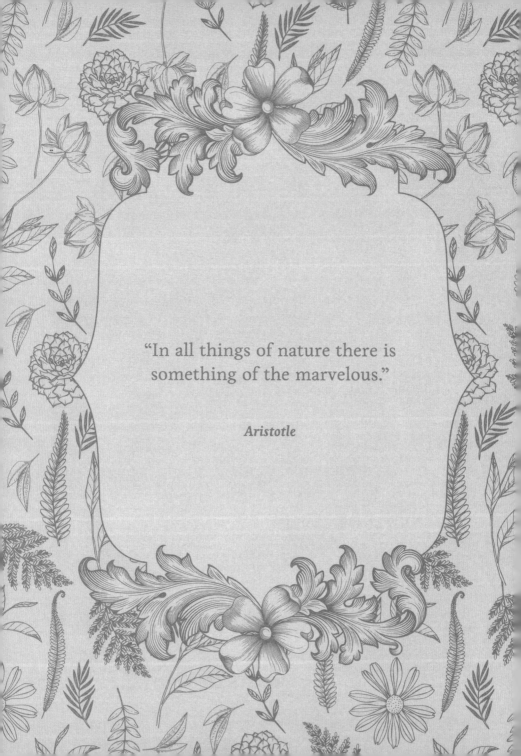

"In all things of nature there is something of the marvelous."

Aristotle

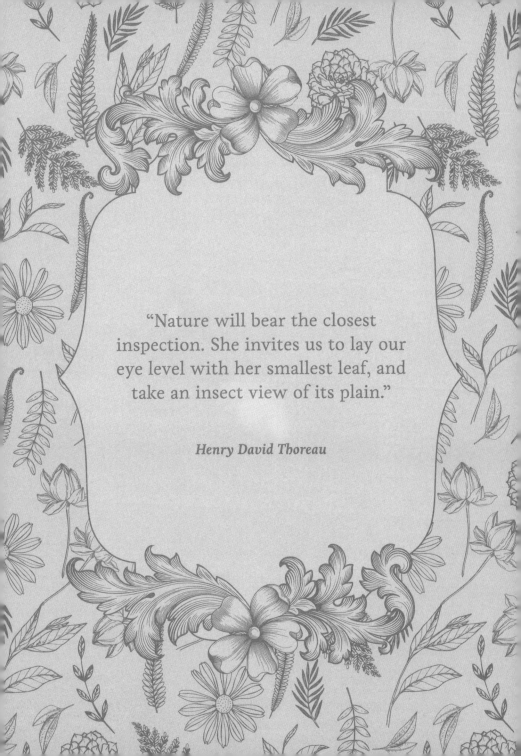

"Nature will bear the closest inspection. She invites us to lay our eye level with her smallest leaf, and take an insect view of its plain."

Henry David Thoreau

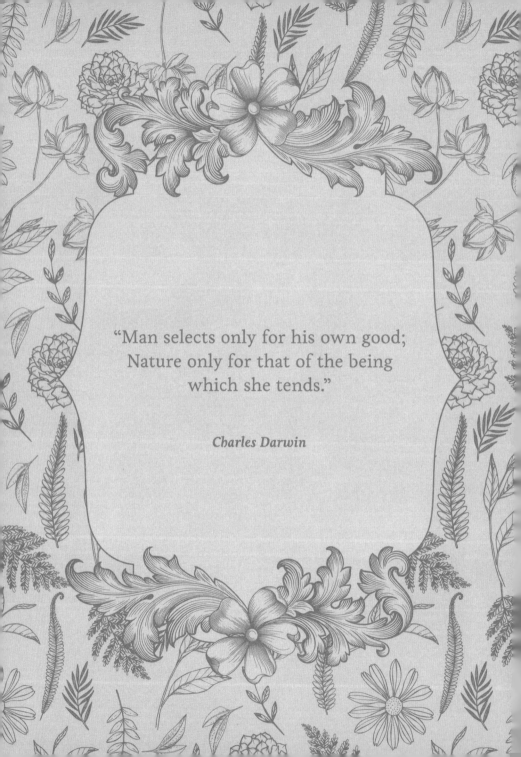

"Man selects only for his own good;
Nature only for that of the being
which she tends."

Charles Darwin

Match the Birds!

Many groupings of birds are called flocks, but plenty of species have much more exciting names when they gather. See how many you can guess correctly.

 Hummingbirds

Murder

Parliament

 Flamingos

 Crows

Gaggle

Flamboyance

 Penguins

Geese

Charm, shimmer

Huddle, rookery

 Eagles

Woodpeckers

Pandemonium

Convocation

 Owls

Cardinals

Descent

Bevy, wedge, lamentation

 Parrots

 Turkeys

College, conclave, radiance

Rafter

 Swans

answers on the next page

Match the Birds!

(answer key)

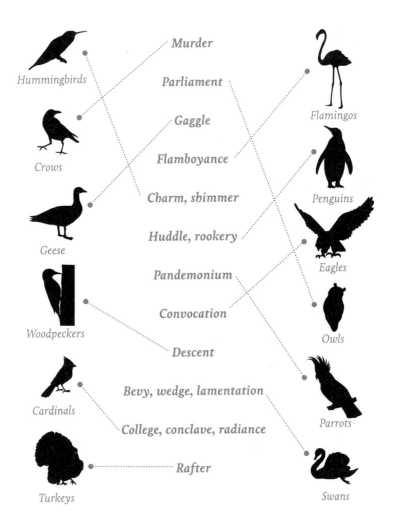

Hummingbirds

Crows

Geese

Woodpeckers

Cardinals

Turkeys

Murder

Parliament

Gaggle

Flamboyance

Charm, shimmer

Huddle, rookery

Pandemonium

Convocation

Descent

Bevy, wedge, lamentation

College, conclave, radiance

Rafter

Flamingos

Penguins

Eagles

Owls

Parrots

Swans

A Botanical Pantry

Herbs make wonderful additions to all kinds of foods, from soups and salads to dressings and sauces. But certain flowers and herbs can also add their own floral essence and flavor to things like syrup and vinegar, which can then be used as additions to desserts, beverages, and vinaigrettes. Here's how you can make your own at home.

INFUSED SYRUPS

Use a splash of your finished syrup in lemonade, iced tea, club soda, tonic water, or your favorite grown-up beverage, even iced coffee.

What you'll need:

- 1 cup (200 g) sugar
- 1 cup (235 ml) water
- Organic flowers, gently washed (see Box, page 36)

- Saucepan
- Fine-mesh strainer
- Bottle or mason jar

What you'll do:

1. In a small saucepan, bring the sugar and water to a simmer. Stir and simmer until the sugar is dissolved, 3 to 5 minutes. Remove from the heat and add the flowers. Cover and set aside for at least one hour and up to twelve to infuse the syrup.

2. Strain into a bottle or mason jar, label, and refrigerate for up to 1 month. Your syrup will take on a lovely hue!

Some edible flowers to try:
Dandelion: ½ (27 g) cup flower petals
Elderflower: ½ (27 g) dozen heads
Hibiscus: 1 cup (54 g) flowers
Lavender: ⅓ cup (18 g) flowers
Rose: 2 cups (108 g) petals
Violet or pansy: 3 cups (162 g) flowers

INFUSED VINEGARS

This is a basic recipe and is easily doubled for larger jars. Use it in place of regular vinegar in any recipe for vinaigrette or sauce that calls for it.

What you'll need:

- 2 cups (470 ml) unpasteurized apple cider vinegar (or any vinegar with 5% acidity)
- 1 cup (about 140 g) fresh organic fruit and/or herbs, gently washed and patted dry (see Box, right)

- Mason jar
- Parchment paper
- Fine-mesh strainer

What you'll do:

1. Chop herbs or fruit and place into a clean mason jar. Pour in the apple cider vinegar to cover, leaving ½ to 1 inch headspace (depending

on the size of your jar and how much vinegar you're using). Wipe off the rim, cover with parchment paper, and put the metal ring on the jar (or use a rubber band or piece of kitchen twine to secure the paper in place). Label the jar and set aside to steep for two to three weeks in a cool dark place. (Periodically, you can add the jar's lid and give the mixture a shake.)

2. Strain with a fine-mesh strainer, pressing down on the fruit and herbs to extract as much vinegar as possible. Transfer infused vinegar to a bottle or clean mason jar, label, and store in the refrigerator for several months.

Some edible plants to try:
Chive blossom heads
Chili peppers
Ginger
Sage, rosemary, thyme, mint, lemon verbena leaves
Dill or fennel heads and fronds
Berries
Chopped stone fruit

Fun with Flornithology

Robert Williams Wood, an American physicist and inventor, took the portmanteau of flora (flowers) and ornithology (the study of birds) to the next level with the publication of his 1907 book *How to Tell the Birds from the Flowers and Other Wood-Cuts: A Manual of Flornithology for Beginners*. In it, he describes, in verse and illustration, 49 delightful nature puns, comparing terns to turnips, gnus to newts, larks to larkspur, and pansies to "chim-pansies." In his introduction, at right, he references Gray (of Henry Gray's *Anatomy of the Human Body*) and Audubon (of John James Audubon's *The Birds of America*) and makes his apologies to all naturalists.

The Jay.

The Bay.

The Blue Jay, as we clearly see,
Is so much like the green Bay tree
That one might say the only clue,
Lies in their dif-fer-ence of hue,
And if you have a color sense,
You'll see at once this difference.

Intro·duc·tion.

By other Nature books I'm sure,
You've often been misled,
You've tried a wall-flower to secure.
And "picked a hen" instead:
You've wondered what the egg-plants lay,
And why the chestnut's burred,
And if the hop-vine hops away,
It's perfectly absurd.
I hence submit for your inspection,
This very new and choice collection,
Of flowers on Storks, and Phlox of birds,
With some explanatory words.
Not every one is always able
To recognize a vegetable,

For some are guided by tradition,
While others use their intuition,
And even I make no pretense
Of having more than common sense.
Indeed these strange homologies
Are in most flornithologies,
And I have freely drawn upon
The works of Gray and Audubon,
Avoiding though the frequent blunders
Of those who study Nature's wonders.

Puffin.   Nuffin.

Upon this cake of ice is perched,
The paddle-footed Puffin:
To find his double I have searched,
But have discovered—Nuffin'.

The Bee. The Beet. The Beetle.

Good Mr. Darwin once contended
That Beetles were from Bees descended,
And as my pictures show I think
The Beet must be the missing link.
The sugar-beet and honey-bee
Supply the Beetle's pedigree:
The family is now complete,—
The Bee, the Beetle and the Beet.

The ELK.   The Whelk.

A roar of welkome through the welkin
Is certain proof you'll find the Elk in;
But if you listen to the shell,
In which the Whelk is said to dwell,
And hear a roar, beyond a doubt
It indicates the Whelk is out.

The Cat-bird.   The Cat-nip.

The Cat-bird's call resembles that
Emitted by the Pussy Cat,
While Cat-nip growing by the wall,
Is never known to caterwaul:
It's odor though attracts the Kits,
And throws them in Cat-nip-tion fits.

Now try your hand at writing verse to Wood's pictures.

The Crow.   The Crocus.

 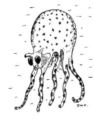

The Puss.   The Octo-pus.

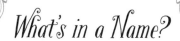

What's in a Name?

Not to be confused with an organism's common name, *binomial nomenclature* is the two-part naming system for all plants, animals, and insects. Developed in 1753 by Swedish biologist Carl von Linne (also known as Linnaeus), it uses Latin to classify all manner of beings.

The first word is the genus and the second is the species, which adds further description to the genus. Sometimes, there's a third word, which denotes cultivar, or a variety. For example, the genus *Canis* encompasses jackals, wolves, and dogs. Adding the species name *lupus* winnows it down to wolves and dogs. Then *Canis lupus familiaris* is reserved for Fido.

Those who have the honor of naming flora and fauna often choose names inspired by Greek and Latin words or myths pertaining to how the species looked/s or what it did/does. Sometimes they name them after themselves or after someone or something in popular culture. And some of the names sound downright silly. Here are a few examples from the plant world. Do you see the connections?

Silybum marianum (milk thistle): *Silybum* comes from the Greek *silybon* or *silybos*, meaning "tassel" or "tuft." The Latin *marianus* refers to Mary, mother of Jesus, and the appearance of white milky spots on the leaves.

Dracaena trifasciata (snake plant, mother-in-law's tongue): _Dracaena_ comes from the Greek _drakaina_, for "female dragon," and _trifasciata_, from the Latin _tri_ for three and _faciatus_, meaning "banded" or "striped," to describe the plant's leaves.

Octospora humosa (hotlips disco): Though this bright orange-red fungus was named "Hotlips" by a girl in the United Kingdom, inspired by its color and shape, its binomial comes from the Latin _octo spora_ ("eight spores") and _humosus_ ("full of humus, of soil").

Monstera deliciosa (Swiss cheese plant): From the Latin _monstera_, for "monstrous" or "abnormal," referring to the holes in its leaves. _Deliciosa_, from the Latin _deliciosus_, means "delicious," referring to its edible fruit.

Ranunculus ophioglossifolius (adder's tongue spearwort): From the Latin _rana_ ("frog") and the diminutive _unculus_, so "little frog," perhaps referring to ranunculus preferring moist soil (as near water, like little frogs). Also, from the Greek _ophis_ ("serpent") and _glossa_ ("tongue"), plus the Latin _folium_ ("leaf").

Ilex vomitoria (Yaupon holly): From the Latin _vomere_, _vomitoria_ is rather self-explanatory, especially as the berries of this plant are poisonous. _Ilex_ refers to the holm oak, which resembles holly.

***Arctostaphylos uva-ursi* (bearberry):** From the Greek *arctos*, meaning "bear," and *staphyle*, meaning "bunch of grapes," referring to its berry clusters. *Uva-ursi* comes from the Latin for "grape" *(uva)* and "bear" *(ursus)*, so really, this plant could be called "bear berry berry-bear."

***Asterophora parasitica* (silky piggyback):** This mushroom grows on the remains of other fungi—a piggyback of sorts—though "parasite" comes from the Latin *parasiticus*. Similarly, *phora* (a form of *phero*) is Greek for "carry."

***Dendrobium bigibbum* (Cooktown orchid):** From the Greek *dendron* for "tree" and *bios* for "life," referring to how orchids grow on trees. *Bigibbum* means "two humped," from the Latin *bi* ("two") and *gibbous* ("hump"), referring to the flower's appearance.

***Chelone lyonii* (pink turtlehead):** From the Greek *chelone* ("turtle" or "tortoise") for the appearance of its flowers; *lyonii* named for Scottish-American horticulturist John Lyon, who is credited with discovering this species in the Southern Appalachians.

***Utricularia gibba* (humped bladderwort):** This aquatic, floating flower is named from the Latin *utriculus* ("wine flask" or "leather bottle") and *gibbus* ("humped").

***Phallus impudicus* (common stinkhorn):** Both words are Latin, and the look of this upright mushroom is quite *impudicus*, for "immodest" or "shameless."

Connect the Dots!

solution on page 174

Connect the Dots!

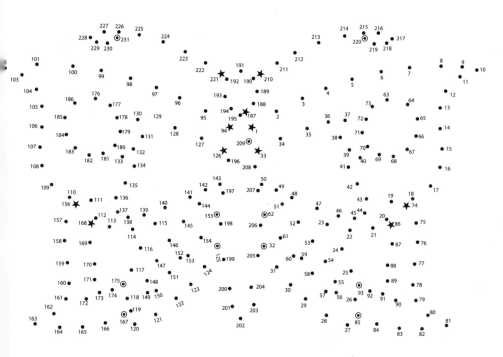

solution on page 175

Nature Trivia I

Each of these is the name of an orchid, except:
- ○ *Polystachya pubescens*
- ○ *Pediomelum tenuiflorum*
- ○ *Paphiopedilum* Doctor Toot
- ○ *Miltoniopsis* Arthur Cobbledick

Who is considered the founder of evolutionary biology?
- ○ Charles Dickens
- ○ Jacques Cousteau
- ○ Charles Darwin
- ○ Steve Irwin

Which species has the greatest population on earth?
- ○ Fish
- ○ Humans
- ○ Birds
- ○ Insects

Which of the following is not a plant in real life?
- ○ Audrey Flytrap
- ○ Creeping Jenny
- ○ Dazzling Stacy
- ○ Sweet William

What differentiates flora from fauna?
- ○ Flora never die; fauna have a lifespan
- ○ Flora can make their own food; fauna must obtain food from outside sources
- ○ Flora lack a cell wall; fauna possess a cell wall
- ○ Flora do not reproduce because they need seeds; fauna reproduce by having offspring

Which of the following are mammals?
- ○ Rhinoceros
- ○ Blue whale
- ○ Beaver
- ○ All of the above

Deathwatch, whirligig, and atlas are types of which insect?
- ○ Moth
- ○ Beetle
- ○ Fly
- ○ Mantis

answers on page 172

Match the Sticker!

answers on page 168

All Hail the Queen (Bee)!

Honeybees (*Apis mellifera*) may just be one type of pollinator (along with butterflies, bats, and birds), but they are vital to life as we know it. According to the U.S. Department of Agriculture, one out of every three bites we eat is thanks to a pollinator. There are more than 3,500 species of native bees that help to put food on our plates, which includes more than 130 types of fruit, vegetables, and nuts.

And let's not forget the honey! It takes 36 worker bees six weeks (nearly their entire lives) to produce 1 tablespoon of honey. Not only does honey taste great on a peanut butter sandwich, in a cup of tea, and chewed as a treat right on the comb, it also holds medicinal properties. It's been found to have antioxidant, antimicrobial, and anti-inflammatory effects (among others) and has been used to manage maladies from sore throats and wounds to asthma, diabetes, and even cancer.

Though there is a natural increase and decrease in the number of bees in a colony over the course of a year, in the past two decades, bee populations have been declining dramatically around the world. Signs point to climate change, disease, habitat loss, and pesticide use. The best thing we can all do to help honeybees thrive is to plant native pollinator plants and avoid pesticides.

Let's Make Lemon Beeswax Candles!

Made by busy bees, beeswax is known for its soft honey color and aroma. It burns cleaner and longer than other waxes. Brighten any room with this amazing combination of nature's most soothing scents.

What you'll need:

- 2 lemons
- Sharp knife
- Citrus spoon
- 4 wooden wicks and mounts
- 3.5 ounces (100 g) beeswax pastilles
- Metal pouring pitcher (a pot you dedicate to candle making, available online or in your local craft store)
- A second pot to make a water bath
- Candy thermometer

What you'll do:

1. Cut the lemons lengthwise and carefully peel the fruit from the rind using a knife and citrus spoon. Avoid puncturing or tearing the rind as this will be the vessel for the wax. When you are finished, the peel should be free of pulp.

2. Place the wooden wicks in the center of each lemon peel.

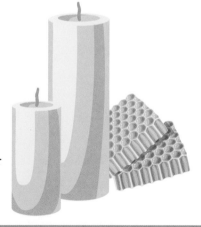

3. Melt the beeswax in a metal pouring pitcher set in a water bath. Once melted, take the wax pot off the heat and allow to cool until the wax is between 140°F and 155°F (60°C–68°C).

4. Pour wax into each of the four lemon halves.

5. Allow to cool fully, four to six hours. Trim the wicks if needed before lighting.

Makes 4 candles

TIP: If you want these lemon candles to have that light, fresh lemon look, use them within 24 hours of making them. After that, the lemon peel will begin to darken and harden (like lemons in potpourri). They still smell great when lit and should not mold since the wax has sealed off all the moisture in the lemon.

Match the Cutie to Its Name!

Baby animals are the cutest, but do you know what they're called? See if you can name these tiny tots.

Kid	Joey	Hoglet	Kit	Cria
Fawn	Infant	Colt	Calf	Fledgling

answers on the next page

Match the Cutie to Its Name!
(answer key)

Hoglet

Joey

Fawn

Calf

Fledgling

Kid

Kit

Cria

Colt

Infant

Match the Marine Animal!

Groupings of fish are often called schools, but so many aquatic creatures have much more colorful names when they get together to have some fun. See how many you can guess correctly.

Sharks

Glide

Dolphins

Shiver

Swordfish

Herd

Crabs

Bale

Pod

Squid

Flotilla

Flying Fish

Sea Turtles

Shoal

Swarm

Jellyfish

Cast

Seahorses

Bloom, swarm, smack

Clams

Fever

Eels

Bed

Stingrays

answers on the next page

Match the Marine Animal!

(answer key)

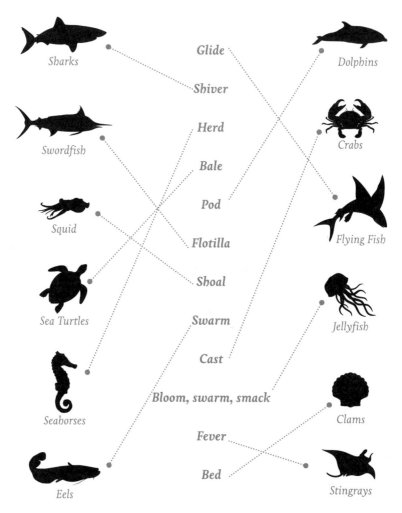

Sharks

Swordfish

Squid

Sea Turtles

Seahorses

Eels

Glide

Shiver

Herd

Bale

Pod

Flotilla

Shoal

Swarm

Cast

Bloom, swarm, smack

Fever

Bed

Dolphins

Crabs

Flying Fish

Jellyfish

Clams

Stingrays

How to Preserve a Bouquet

Whether you handpicked a bunch of wildflower stems, cut some blooms from your own garden, or received a gorgeous bouquet as a gift, there's no reason the flowers need to go into the compost pile (or worse, the trash!). It's easy to preserve your bouquet to keep as its own decoration, or preserve groups of flowers for later use in potpourri or sachets or in crafts such as bath salts, candles, and wreaths. The simplest way to do this is by air drying them.

What you'll need:

- Flowers, stripped of excess foliage (see page 108)
- Flower snips or sharp scissors
- Twine or rubber bands

What you'll do:

1. Trim the stems, leaving at least 6 inches (15 cm). Arrange in a pleasing bunch of 8 to 10 stems; you might have to divide a larger bouquet. Tie the stems together with the twine or rubber band.

2. Hang the bouquet upside down in a dark, dry, well-ventilated place until dried, two to three weeks.

3. Once dried, take down the flowers and spray with unscented hairspray to protect them. If using for later craft purposes, you may keep them hanging upside down until needed or wrap them loosely in craft paper and store in a box.

> If you're picking the flowers yourself, the best time to do it is in the morning just before the blooms open completely.

Here are some flowers and plants that would be suitable for drying in bunches; you'll have more success with flowers that hold their petals tightly and have small green leaves at their base (the calyx). Interestingly, the Victorians assigned meanings to flowers so they could subtly send messages to friends and paramours. The meanings here come from the 1884 book *Language of Flowers* by Kate Greenaway—but don't let the meanings get in your way. Beauty is in the eye of the beholder, after all.

ROSE *red for bashful, red rosebud for pure and lovely, white for "I am worthy of you," yellow for jealousy, decrease of love*

DWARF SUNFLOWER
adoration

AMARANTH
(Globe) immortality, unfading love

RUDBECKIA *justice*

FERN *fascination*

CRESS *stability, power*

EVERLASTING
*never-ceasing
remembrance*

SAGE *esteem*

LARKSPUR
lightness, levity

LOVE IN A MIST
perplexity

What Is Your *Scientific Name?*

Match the first letter of your first name with the first list of words. Match the first letter of your last name with the second list. Match your birthday with the genus name in the third list on page 112. Perhaps your name will create an exciting new species!

Introducing

A	*Alba* (white)		A	*Alatus* (winged)
B	*Cyano* (blue)		B	*Barbatus* (bearded)
C	*Campanula* (bell-shaped)		C	*Caulis* (stemmed)
D	*Diplo* (double)		D	*Digitatus* (fingered, toed)
E	*Erythro* (red)		E	*Echinatus* (prickly, spiny)
F	*Fili* (threadlike)		F	*Formosus* (beautiful, well-formed)
G	*Gracili* (slender)		G	*Gracilipes* (slender-footed)
H	*Hirtus* (hairy)		H	*Hamatus* (hooked)
I	*Incana* (grey)		I	*Irregularis* (unusual, irregular)
J	*Gymno* (naked)		J	*Jubatus* (crested, maned)
K	*Gala* (milky)		K	*Gibbus* (humped)
L	*Lithos* (stone)		L	*Laetus* (pleasant, delighted)
M	*Melano* (black)		M	*Megacephalus* (big-headed)
N	*Nocti* (of the night)		N	*Nitidus* (shining, bright)
O	*Ortho* (upright, straight)		O	*Obscurus* (dark)
P	*Platy* (broad, flat)		P	*Plumosum* (feathered, feathery)
Q	*Suavis* (sweet)		Q	*Fasciatus* (striped)
R	*Reptans* (creeping, crawling)		R	*Rostratus* (beaked, having a beak)
S	*Strepto* (twisted)		S	*Squamatus* (scaled, scaly)
T	*Trachy* (rough, rugged)		T	*Tomentosus* (furry)
U	*Hypo* (under)		U	*Ulos* (woolly)
V	*Viridi* (green)		V	*Virosus* (poisonous, rank)
W	*Pendula* (weeping, hanging)		W	*Xylic* (wooden)
X	*Xero* (dry)		X	*Rigidus* (rigid, stiff)
Y	*Flavi* (yellow)		Y	*Setosus* (bristly, shaggy)
Z	*Maculata* (spotted)		Z	*Zygos* (joined, paired)

1	*Canis* (dog, wolf, coyote)	17	*Panthera* (lion, tiger, jaguar, leopard)
2	*Pinus* (pine tree)	18	*Rosa* (rose)
3	*Equus* (horse, zebra)	19	*Elephas* (elephant)
4	*Bulbophyllum* (orchid)	20	*Cereus* (cactus)
5	*Octopus*	21	*Strix* (owl)
6	*Acer* (maple tree)	22	*Hedera* (ivy)
7	*Anas* (duck)	23	*Aquila* (eagle)
8	*Tulipa* (tulip)	24	*Lilium* (lily)
9	*Apis* (bee)	25	*Hydrochoerus* (capybara)
10	*Taraxacum* (dandelion)	26	*Actinidia* (kiwifruit)
11	*Felis* (cat)	27	*Aptenodytes* (great penguin)
12	*Malus* (apple)	28	*Paeonia* (peony)
13	*Testudo* (tortoise)	29	*Naja* (cobra)
14	*Asplenium* (fern)	30	*Ficus* (banyan tree, fig)
15	*Crocodilia* (crocodile)	31	*Bos* (ox, cow)
16	*Cucumis* (melon, cucumber)		

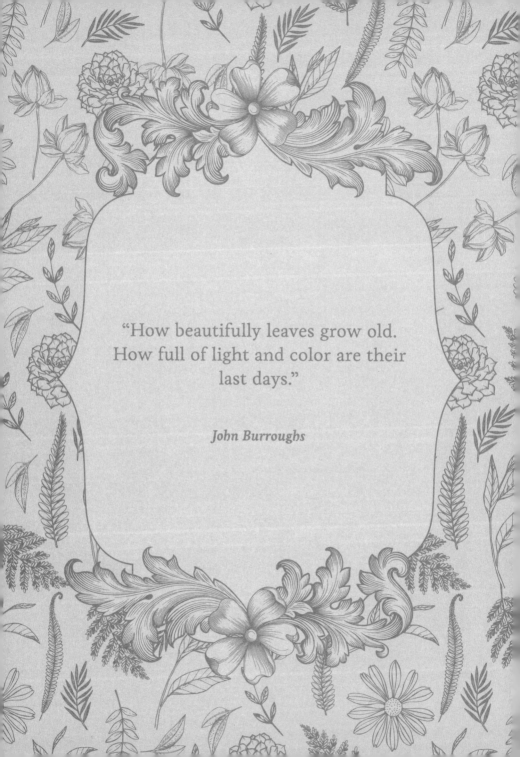

"How beautifully leaves grow old.
How full of light and color are their
last days."

John Burroughs

Caption This!

Match the Sticker!

answers on page 170

Sudoku

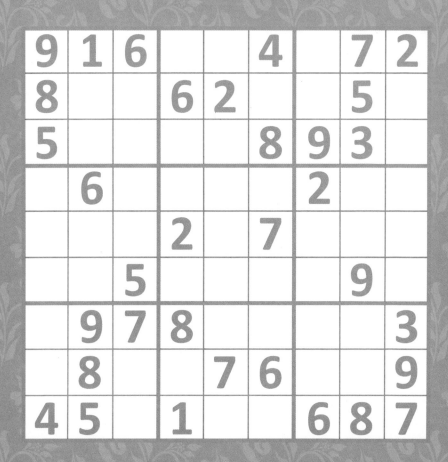

solution on page 176

Nature Trivia II

All of these are characteristics of mammals, except:
- O They have a backbone
- O They produce milk
- O Their blood temperature fluctuates
- O They birth live young

What is the name of a person who studies butterflies?
- O Entomologist
- O Lepidopterist
- O Phytologist
- O Mycologist

What is the two-part naming system to classify living organisms?
- O Xylem and phloem
- O Organic permaculture
- O Double helix
- O Binomial nomenclature

What is the largest tree on earth (by volume)?
- O Banyan tree
- O Giant sequoia
- O Montezuma cypress
- O Bristlecone pine

What is the process by which a species adapts to its surroundings?
- O Nature versus nurture
- O Biotic factor
- O Natural selection
- O Biology

What makes a platypus unique among mammals?
- O It lays eggs
- O It swims underwater
- O It carries its young in a pouch
- O It has water-repellant fur

answers on page 173

Sudoku

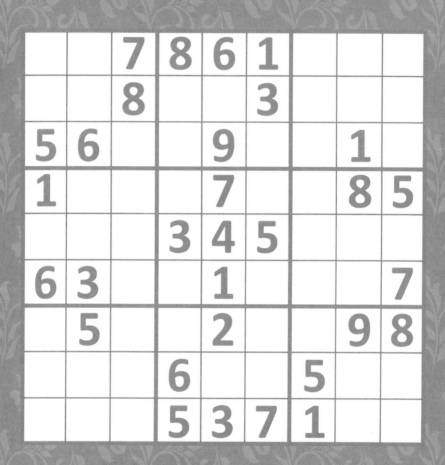

solution on page 176

Binomial Namesakes

Sometimes, scientists who discover a new species name it for people (real or fictional) because of a certain influence or resemblance, and sometimes, it's just a cool name. Match the flora or fauna's scientific name in the left column to the lightly cloaked namesake in the right.

_____	*Achillea millefolium*	A. *The Hobbit*'s dragon
_____	*Alphomelon simpsonorum*	B. Nashville singer
_____	*Amblyrhynchus cristatus godzilla*	C. Pooh's bouncing friend
_____	*Bagheera kiplingi*	D. Ziggy Stardust
_____	*Craspedotropis gretathunbergae*	E. Springfield's cartoon family
_____	*Danionella dracula*	F. 007
_____	*Dracula smaug*	G. Keeper of the Precious
_____	*Elseya irwini*	H. Trojan War hero
_____	*Gollum suluensis*	I. Swedish eco-activist
_____	*Heteropoda davidbowie*	J. Conan Doyle's sleuth
_____	*Japewiella dollypartoniana*	K. Shakespeare's fairy royalty
_____	*Mandevilla sherlockii*	L. BBC naturalist
_____	*Monodelphis pinocchio*	M. Resident of Bikini Bottom
_____	*Nepenthes attenboroughii*	N. Japanese monster
_____	*Oberonia titania*	O. Gotham City's hero
_____	*Otocinclus batmani*	P. Sesame Street's grump
_____	*Potamalpheops tigger*	Q. Mowgli's mentor
_____	*Pterichis aragogiana*	R. Bram Stoker's villain
_____	*Simlops jamesbondi*	S. Australian animal lover
_____	*Spongiforma squarepantsii*	T. Hagrid's pet spider
_____	*Stelis oscargrouchii* Karremans	U. Geppetto's wooden boy

answers on the next page

Binomial Namesakes

(answer key)

H	*A. millefolium* (yarrow)	**Trojan War:** Achilles
E	*A. simpsonorum* (wasp)	**Springfield:** the Simpsons
N	*A. cristatus godzilla* (iguana)	**Japanese monster:** Godzilla
Q	*B. kiplingi* (spider)	**Mowgli's mentor:** Bagheera
I	*C. gretathunbergae* (snail)	**Swedish eco:** Greta Thunberg
R	*D. dracula* (fish)	**Bram Stoker's villain:** Dracula
A	*D. smaug* (orchid)	**Hobbit's dragon:** Smaug
S	*E. irwini* (turtle)	**Australian:** Steve Irwin
G	*G. suluensis* (shark)	**Keeper of Precious:** Gollum
D	*H. davidbowie* (spider)	**Ziggy Stardust:** David Bowie
B	*J. dollypartoniana* (lichen)	**Nashville:** Dolly Parton
J	*M. sherlockii* (mandevilla)	**Conan Doyle:** Sherlock Holmes
U	*M. pinocchio* (opossum)	**Geppetto's boy:** Pinocchio
L	*N. attenboroughii* (pitcher plant)	**BBC:** Sir David Attenborough
K	*O. titania* (orchid)	**Shakespeare:** Oberon & Titania
O	*O. batmani* (catfish)	**Gotham's hero:** Batman
C	*P. tigger* (shrimp)	**Pooh's friend:** Tigger
T	*P. aragogiana* (orchid)	**Hagrid's spider:** Aragog
F	*S. jamesbondi* (spider)	**007:** James Bond
M	*S. squarepantsii* (fungus)	**Resident:** Spongebob Squarepants
P	*S. oscargrouchii* (orchid)	**Sesame:** Oscar the Grouch

Match the Amphibian, Reptile, and Insect!

Whether a grouping of these creatures brings you joy or gives you nightmares, their collective names are rather appropriate. See how many you can guess correctly.

Crocodiles

Army

Bask, float

Snakes

Creep

Iguanas

Mess

Tortoises

Den, pit, bed

Mosquitoes

Drift, hive

Frogs

Colony

Snails

Kaleidoscope

Ants

Cloud

Bees

Cluster, clutter

Butterflies

Swarm

Grasshoppers

Walk

Spiders

answers on the next page

Match the Amphibian, Reptile, and Insect!

(answer key)

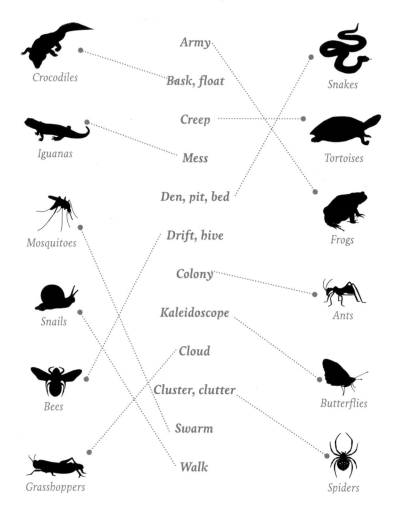

Crocodiles

Army

Bask, float

Creep

Mess

Snakes

Iguanas

Tortoises

Den, pit, bed

Drift, hive

Frogs

Mosquitoes

Colony

Kaleidoscope

Ants

Snails

Cloud

Cluster, clutter

Butterflies

Bees

Swarm

Walk

Grasshoppers

Spiders

Complete the Image

Scavenger Hunt

Exploring nature can be as simple as peering out a window, but getting outside brings all the senses into play. Sometimes we're too busy to "stop and smell the roses," when we don't take in everything around us. Go outside and check off all that you find.

○ Mushroom or lichen

○ Cobweb

○ Tree nut (chestnut, acorn, etc.)

○ Pinecone or needles

○ Red leaf

○ Yellow leaf

○ Sparkly stone

○ Crooked stick

○ Black bird

○ Blue flower

○ Ladybug

○ Bumble bee

○ Anthill

○ Butterfly or moth

○ Animal tracks or prints

○ Puddle

○ Worm

○ Squirrel

○ Rabbit

○ Dandelion

○ Feather

○ Smooth rock

○ Moss

○ Dirt or sand

solution on page 166

solution on page 167

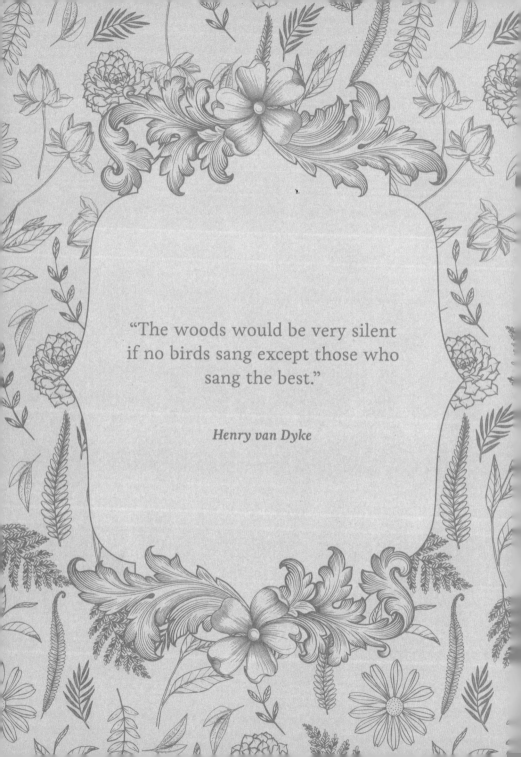

"The woods would be very silent
if no birds sang except those who
sang the best."

Henry van Dyke

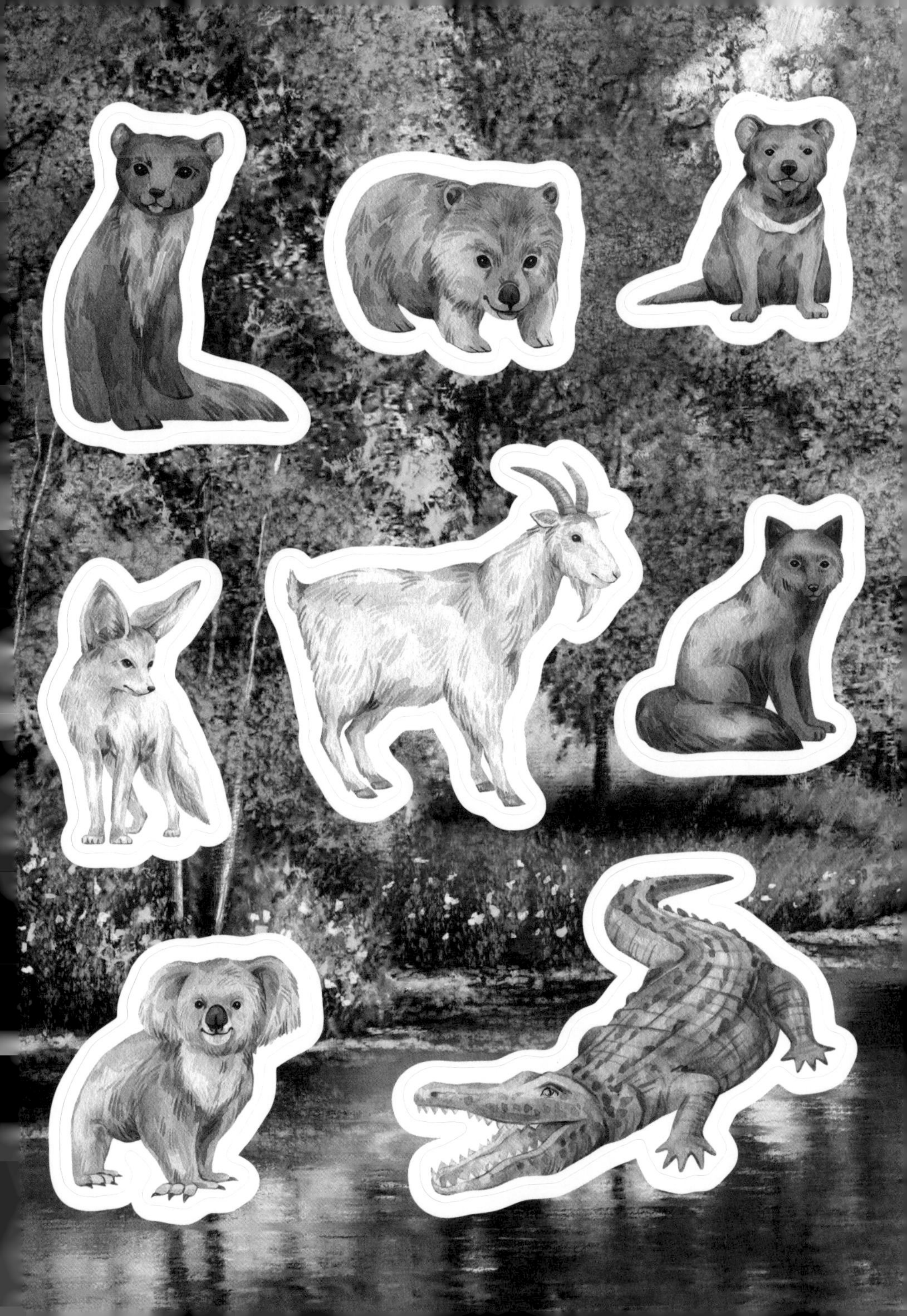

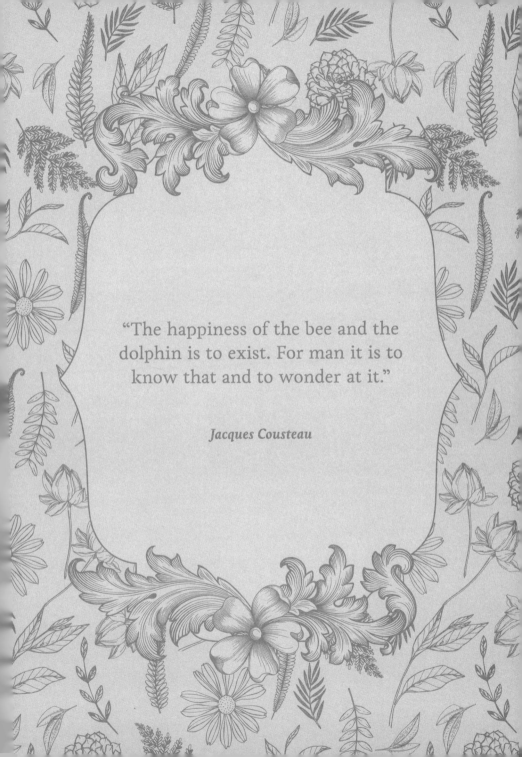

"The happiness of the bee and the dolphin is to exist. For man it is to know that and to wonder at it."

Jacques Cousteau

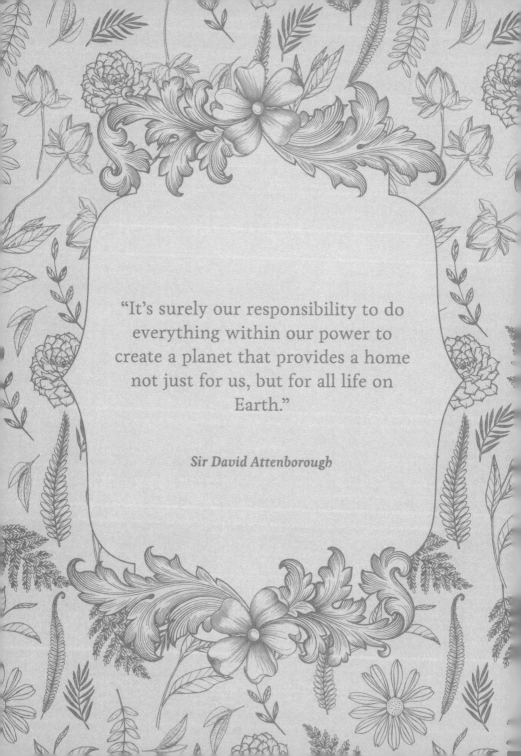

"It's surely our responsibility to do everything within our power to create a planet that provides a home not just for us, but for all life on Earth."

Sir David Attenborough

maze on page 8

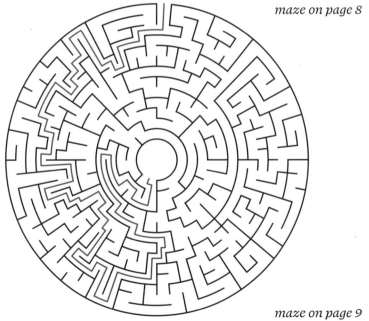

maze on page 9

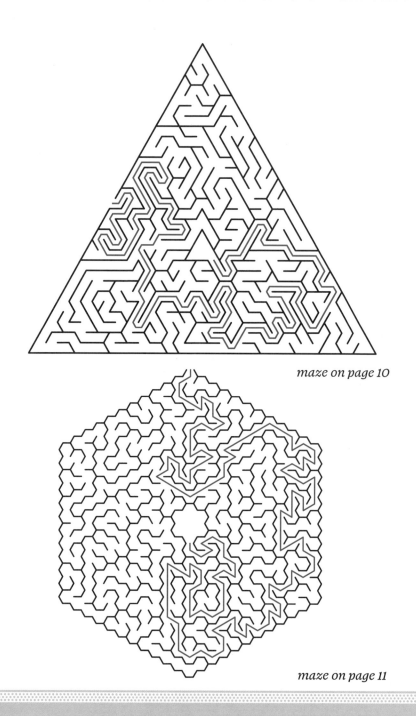

maze on page 10

maze on page 11

maze on page 12

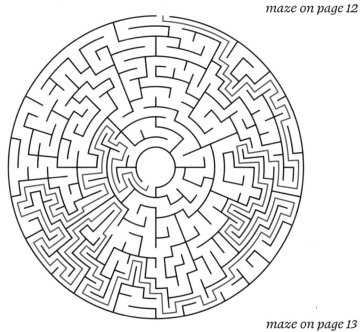

maze on page 13

maze on page 14

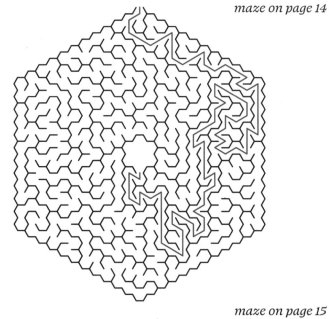

maze on page 15

maze on page 16

maze on page 142

maze on page 143

Match the Sticker!
(answer key)

sticker on page 114

sticker on page 26

sticker on page 87

sticker on page 86

sticker on page 83

sticker on page 26

sticker on page 87

sticker on page 86

puzzle on page 98

Match the Sticker!
(answer key)

sticker on page 54

sticker on page 94

sticker on page 151

sticker on page 122

sticker on page 95

sticker on page 23

puzzle on page 130

Nature Trivia I (answer key)

Each of these is the name of an orchid, except:
○ *Polystachya pubescens*
☑ *Pediomelum tenuiflorum*
○ *Paphiopedilum* Doctor Toot
○ *Miltoniopsis* Arthur Cobbledick

Who is considered the founder of evolutionary biology?
○ Charles Dickens
○ Jacques Cousteau
☑ Charles Darwin
○ Steve Irwin

Which species has the greatest population on earth?
○ Fish
○ Humans
○ Birds
☑ Insects

Which of the following is not a plant in real life?
☑ Audrey Flytrap
○ Creeping Jenny
○ Dazzling Stacy
○ Sweet William

What differentiates flora from fauna?
○ Flora never die; fauna have a lifespan
☑ Flora can make their own food; fauna must obtain food from outside sources
○ Flora lack a cell wall; fauna possess a cell wall
○ Flora do not reproduce because they need seeds; fauna reproduce by having offspring

Which of the following are mammals?
○ Rhinoceros
○ Blue whale
○ Beaver
☑ All of the above

Deathwatch, whirligig, and atlas are types of which insect?
○ Moth
☑ Beetle
○ Fly
○ Mantis

trivia on page 48

Nature Trivia II (answer key)

All of these are characteristics of mammals, except:
- ○ They have a backbone
- ○ They produce milk
- ☑ Their blood temperature fluctuates
- ○ They birth live young

What is the name of a person who studies butterflies?
- ○ Entomologist
- ☑ Lepidopterist
- ○ Phytologist
- ○ Mycologist

What is the two-part naming system to classify living organisms?
- ○ Xylem and phloem
- ○ Organic permaculture
- ○ Double helix
- ☑ Binomial nomenclature

What is the largest tree on earth (by volume)?
- ○ Banyan tree
- ☑ Giant sequoia
- ○ Montezuma cypress
- ○ Bristlecone pine

What is the process by which a species adapts to its surroundings?
- ○ Nature versus nurture
- ○ Biotic factor
- ☑ Natural selection
- ○ Biology

What makes a platypus unique among mammals?
- ☑ It lays eggs
- ○ It swims underwater
- ○ It carries its young in a pouch
- ○ It has water-repellant fur

trivia on page 133

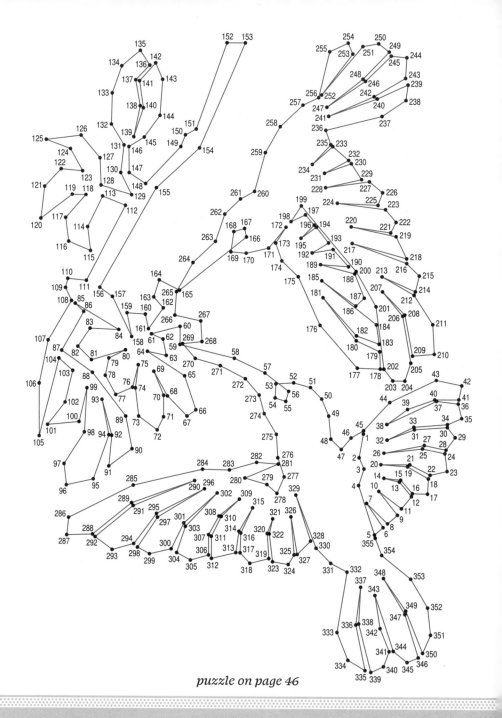

puzzle on page 46

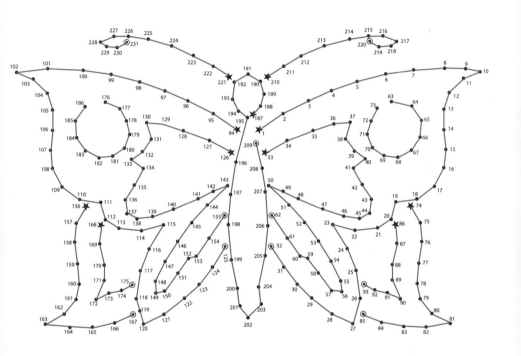

puzzle on page 47

Sudoku (answer key)

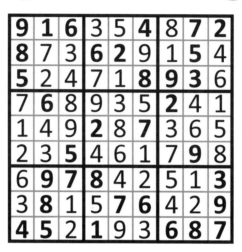

9	1	6	3	5	4	8	7	2
8	7	3	6	2	9	1	5	4
5	2	4	7	1	8	9	3	6
7	6	8	9	3	5	2	4	1
1	4	9	2	8	7	3	6	5
2	3	5	4	6	1	7	9	8
6	9	7	8	4	2	5	1	3
3	8	1	5	7	6	4	2	9
4	5	2	1	9	3	6	8	7

puzzle on page 132

9	4	7	8	6	1	2	5	3
2	1	8	4	5	3	6	7	9
5	6	3	7	9	2	8	1	4
1	9	4	2	7	6	3	8	5
7	8	2	3	4	5	9	6	1
6	3	5	9	1	8	4	2	7
3	5	6	1	2	4	7	9	8
4	7	1	6	8	9	5	3	2
8	2	9	5	3	7	1	4	6

puzzle on page 134

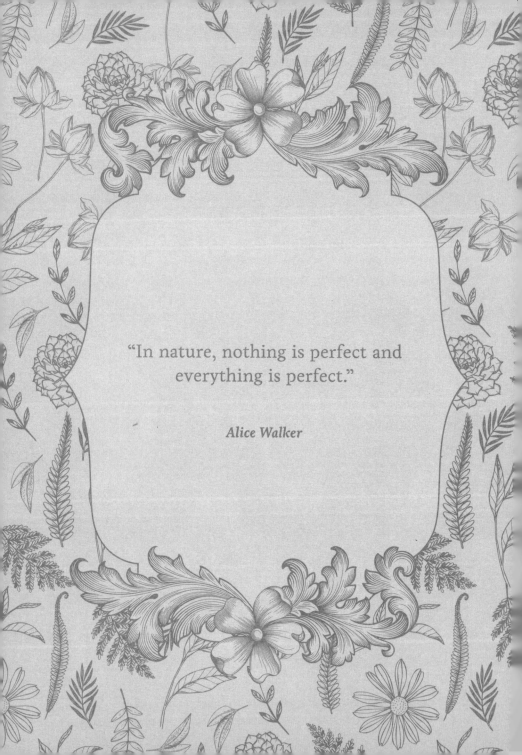

"In nature, nothing is perfect and everything is perfect."

Alice Walker

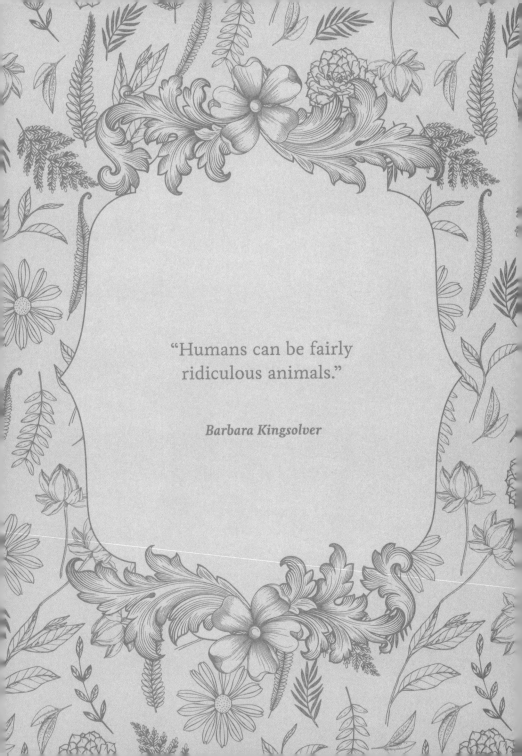

"Humans can be fairly
ridiculous animals."

Barbara Kingsolver

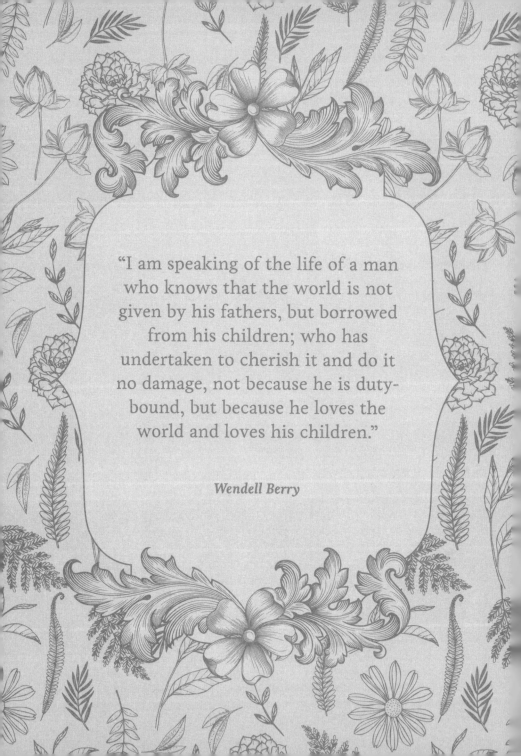

"I am speaking of the life of a man who knows that the world is not given by his fathers, but borrowed from his children; who has undertaken to cherish it and do it no damage, not because he is duty-bound, but because he loves the world and loves his children."

Wendell Berry

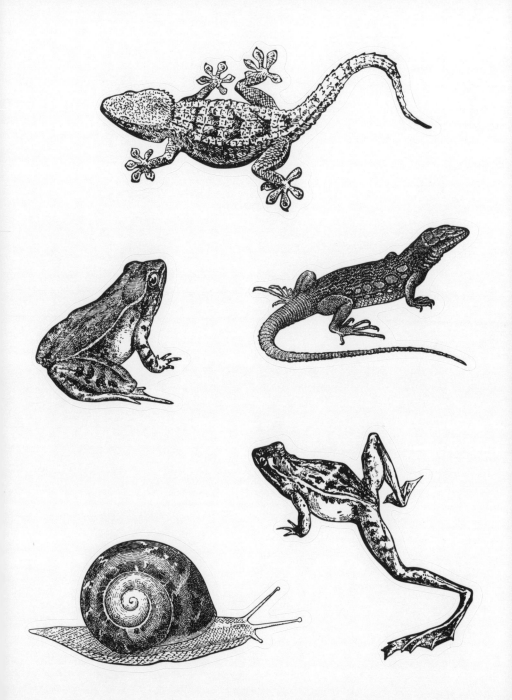